don't look for
your own head

A poetry collection by Meghan Bay

Copyright © 2022 Meghan Bay

All rights reserved.

ISBN 978-1-7388030-0-2

*For the ones who have felt confined,
by the person they want to be.*
x

surrender to the poet

it's easy to let yourself drift
to look in the mirror
and see your head shift
fall off your neck
and into a box
you hear a click
and the universe pops.
all that is left
is the way you think
pressed in your stomach
flooding in ink
ooze from your teeth
stains,
then they shrink.
they'll tell you the ways
of how to forget
pressed to your mouth
like it's a threat.
don't you dare
let bourbon lose depth.
distinction
between worlds
is dispersing.
daring to exist
with only my body.
there's power in an ache
for a lost mind.
should i write a confession
or did i get it all wrong
could i write all my sins
or would sunday move along.
the wicked never waits
for the hungry
i was eager for a feast
now the devil has outdone me.
brittle ego holds in prayers
knowing it's the key.
don't let the repent begin
the adolescent scare
will never let
the gods win

birthmarks

i see how mother
put birthmarks in the sky
the single dash
beneath the moon.
i close my eyes
under the nights freckles
and think of you.
i see how mother
put you in the sky
in shooting stars
and satellites,
in the counting
of constellations
i will try
and close my eyes
but still i think of you.
i see how mother
put birthmarks in the sky
but i wonder why
intoxication seems like an
obligation.
may my lungs bear with me
because still i think of you.
i see how mother
put you in the sky
with the star that streaks
through midnight
and i know
my wish didn't come true
because still
i think of you

juvenile love

teared up eyes
don't be surprised
i never was the best of a lover
its a sugar sweet trap
my mind will be snapped
with the bitterness
that once was another's
to know an existence
outside of this room
you could paint me
a whole other colour
for time's mind is its own
when you're touched
by the hands of another

misplaced time

days go by quick
when time is corrupt
my mind has skipped minutes
thrown laughter in the bin
along with some sanity
how long has there been
two of you
i see doubles
six lives
cats get nine
i deserve a few more
another round please
another
another.
i see memories in silence
but it tarnishes clocks
and i beg of god
to make feelings stop.
time deserves none of me
it plays games with me
makes fun of me
mama why do they laugh at me
"they don't my dear; you do"
its hysterical,
the way they look at me
widen those teeth for me.
i take another drink
i wake up tomorrow
they tell me what they think
those are the thoughts i borrow
often i know it wont last
but it seems endless.
and to recognize
i was once
a twelve years old girl
dreaming
of being a drunk
and reckless poet.
sometimes it worried me
but often times
it felt like life was free.

nauseated love

nausea
you root from the head
i could say i'm sick
or in love instead.
tongues take or give
all the meaning
feet don't step, they just lean
with something he said.
taste sugar as blood
on the tip of the bed.
it's not that we're all going crazy
it's that loves soon to be dead
as a winter old daisy.
it's always good to be tasteful
but he tastes so bitter
in a way that it's graceful.
fill my head to the rim
until he walks me thin.
if he takes a step near
my lips will smear
across the floorboards
leaking out dismay

morning ritual

the first thing i do when i wake
is look in the mirror
and clean two mouths.
and try not to stare
at the teeth i've knocked out
that nobody tried to see

i never expected them to open my jaw
but they showed me a muzzle when i tried
so i collected affection i defied
and stitched fabric love in my stomach

i never knew better
though, he told me from above
my mama did too, but i walked out
because the truth danced
with her enmity

a match was lit on my growth
"an introduction to fate"
my fingers still blister and twinge
when i attempt to baptize myself

i got to the bottom of the other side.

when i roll out of bed
i roll up the dead
and bring myself back to life.

fill my mug with cinnamon coffee
allow the sun to seize my body

i'm not sure if i believe in hell
but i'm sure i'm not there
right now. and even if i'm on my way
there is still a heaven, to so i pray

for each morning i see palm trees sway
in a brighter hue
than they introduced me to.

they still pray for light
when everything they see is white

the birds are poets too
they compile rhythm and recite it
i always knew we got along
but as a kid they would ignite it.
disturbed by my aching wings

when matches are struck
royalty is shifted.
strays mould an empire
from burnt twigs
and knocked out teeth

the first thing i do when i wake
is look out the window
and am reminded
i have built a warped heaven

with two hands and a mind
admiring the light of wildfires

deliberately falling

rain falls
on my crawling bones
that beg for salvation

the cold sting lingers
into crisp summer days.
blinks tireless like i do

you can hear the petrichor
as it taps the top of the shed,
drips sparingly onto me

it pinches my whole body
doesn't categorize into the alphabet
it doesn't let me be a poet

rain falls
and it gets dark after lunch
each morning reeks of vertigo
as i count days to get to zero

habits tell me where to go.
everything turns to a still flag in the wind
now that euphoria puts me low

although rain brought the blues
it was always clear
i just didn't want to know

emerge to disrupt

there's respect in mindful havoc.
mad men see it as a state of disorder
they ask about disposition
then look through like it's vague

i have a lot of questions
one hundred narrows to one.
whats beneath the clowns face?

chaotic manor tucks me in silk sheets
lays my head with dawn.
alters my perception
before i'm even gone

tough men don't know
where they've been
it's not here or down there
never beneath skin

no extension to the parallel
or terror, when their hand reaches.

i recollect the butterfly or snake
emerge or disrupt, devoured in flux

the definition never was the meaning.
running to relapse
is to dig in with keys
locking heads on straight

keep royalty on their knees.
let greed know it's fate

you either define it
or reside yourself to the ache

why cause a brawl against liberty
when you'll always
buy tickets to the circus

saints on sidelines

when i open the door
into the night
i chase the sunrise

aim for first place
always a winner
a continuous sinner
for the holy

for the emergence
of grace

a little in your face
but it's for the wicked

the beautiful
and wide ranged
who maneuver the rise
and don't pretend

a saint
is what you'd say
but they mistake the meaning
for the renegade

the ones who close their eyes
like they've baptized the guidelines
foot on the gas down the sidelines

and as the sun keeps surprising
my objective is rising
i lost what i knew
it goes down to thinking
about, one two

and if we knew
how to experience
more than an illustration
of reality, to begin with

we understand more now
it lent us to liberty
some could say
it was to shrivel me

but to dispose of chivalry
is where it begins

symphony of impressions

we're all under some sort of impression
and when it comes down to it
you've got empathy
and sympathy
you've got the symphony of love
you've got the inner jitters
for the bones of the bitter
is it to tarnish the mind
or develop it?
we're on a trip
we've already crashed a few times
we're on a spaceship
we've already smashed a few lines
or rolled our notions in a spliff.
intoxicated
on bits of the brains
you'll learn a few times
cabernet surely does stain.
to reminisce the child's bliss
of my first kiss
to a wine glass
you'll never know
what you've missed
when it's all the same.
we're all on drugs
some come in capsules
others in vexations
it's a world full of alterations
either hesitation
or imagination
with all the ruinous pride
where do we find creation?
can't they just tell me
where to find my blood
is it in the psychedelic squares
or is it deep in love.
we depend on the restraint
to nourish us
it's an alteration on its own
and it far from worries us

because it's the system
that's been sewn.
life is meant to evoke novelty
we've been searching so long
for this honesty
and if all this time
we had known
there would be no stories to tell.
it's about going somewhere
to stand on the other side for a while.
it really is nothing more
than an impression
if anything, the proper word
is suppression
to do it deliberately
is the eye of the artist
the obsession.
it seems to be
that what we need
is never in two eyes

absent evolution

movement in each day
we forgot the development
and the deficit of each one.
we all evolve in different ways
there was shame in our entity
we took existence out of identity.
who have we become now
are we just done now
always telling you to grow up
then asking where the kids go.
where are the humans
the drunk ones; the corrupt ones
of the gods; of the anarchy
we took the days now
disposed of them
we took the ways but how
we didn't believe in them.
so we changed it
and maintained it
the people at home tell us
we're insane, but
i think we are the only ones
who haven't gone mental.
this world has become so
unsentimental
so full of nostalgia
where is the time to come.
it's gone now.
has been for so long now
preach for herself
understand true wealth
of the criminals.
they never took love
'cause they knew
what it was made of
of years changing gears
of the automatic of the clutch.
to all the men do they know
what they've done
i did it too

but i held the gun.
the absolute halo
an angel of the death
another religion
of the deceased.
i've got loyalty to the uproar
we are the royalty
they didn't ask for
it's ignorance, its bliss
to them it's the abyss.
they can't look past the hunger
with all the outlaw
is a withdrawal
this is who we've become
over the years what the outcome
when we wake up from the dream

raised by caterpillars

it was easy to lose where i belonged
when i've been told creatures like us
don't get to roam over rivers and trees
just chew up leaves and spit them out.

they got mad when i stored them in my stomach
said it would rumble and i'd lose all i've known.
i was too naive to perceive, banality from beliefs

but i brought myself up better
to know we stretch our limbs to grow.
it was easy to lose all i've known

in that theres room to stretch too thin
i did everything i could to abuse distance.
filled my tummy and brain, with alternate existence

terrified i'd get caught up in their beliefs
if i complied for a single day.
there was resistance, deeper than the bone.

wrap myself up in the world behind my eyes
until i could see the bottom of the other side
the ones where my arms spread wide
and a bullet couldn't make me cry

creatures like us are meant to wrap ourselves
in everything we might know
and not to live there.
but to use those encounters as a chrysalis
so maybe one day we can roam

we are going

i never know the route
cause i never really looked
i found much more interest
on how i perceived
than what i was perceiving.
the red lights
slightly press into my chest
so i know we have slowed.
the green lights too
but only on short turns.
and sometimes when you're right
you'll perceive more than the rest.
not to say there's less truth
where they reside
we're just aligned
for different hunts.
it's night time now
and we drive back in our taxis
tipped off sobriety
admiring the sun present
shrivelled rain drops
into the elation
of never knowing
where we'll end up

poet's dignity

when i was eight i would shoot toy guns
to inhale the remaining smoke

i'd buy popeye candy cigarettes
i didn't like the taste

nor the cinnamon whiskey
yet it stuck with me

lingered through my fingers in
the deep west

i thrive for the bottom
of the other side

and i got there, nearly died
nearly

i don't cry anymore
i forgot how. in search for myself

i only found what i'm not
created worth from what i wasn't taught

i burned. carrying a name that wasn't mine
quietly sitting in my crime

at least i can say i fought
for the dignity of being a headless poet

fast forward

i quit each morning
and each night
as i spin towards the sunrise
i ache to close my eyes

it's a shame we destruct in it
as a kid i had trust in it.
what's the fuss
with the alteration

turns out it was lust
for the carbonation
of page numbers
to bubble out of rust

i didn't check the mines
there's no jewel
like the ebony nights
i've seen scatter by

to taper the mind with the enemy
is how you come alive

if only i knew i already died
the first time
i rolled my eyes back

i know you're there

head rests on the velour pillow
a blue so nearly ebony
it matches the sky

for the first time in years.
palms pressed together

sometimes you know
you can't always run

i'm still a kid
in questions of
when mama's cabinet
turned to a rattlesnake

a taste of cinnamon or liquorice
slithered into a world unknown.
dissolving a heart of fragments

what i've come to learn i owe
is always so forsaken.

i stay quiet these days
for they're so mistaken
on why i play the fool

the same words have different definitions
determined on the eyes of prey

head rests on the velour pillow
as i watch the rain fall
for the first time in years
i press my palms together.

the writer grasps much more
in a crooked stream
so god i ask of you
don't do it all for me

purple prints

in the mornings i wish i was a poet
so i turn the kettle on
and use the leftover weed
ground up on the kitchen counter.
thumbs slither back and forth
on the index to form a cylinder
then tucked, tongue slithers
hot water poured over cheap green tea.
i go into the backyard
and sit in my macrame swing
hanging beneath prayer flags
and grapevines,
overlooking dried grass
and limp banana branches.
i spark the lighter
and inhale as i watch
my cat rustle the olive tree.
step on mulberries with petite paws
and fill them with thorns.
a sweetness squished with agony
maybe muses conceal
in cryptic emotions, trickling up
like lust and its first touch.
in the mornings i wish i was a poet
so i sit there writing
writers write, writers write
writers write, writers write
for the rest of the morning
with a spliff losing its patience
and purple footprints
on the concrete

writers write

writers write
writers write
writers
write
writers write
writers write writers
write writers write
writers write
writers
write
writers write
writers write writers
write writers write writers
write writers
write writers write
writers
write
writers write
writers write writers
write writers write
writers
write
writers
write
writers write
writers write writers
write writers
write write write
writers write writers
write
writers write
writers write
write write
write
write

do i know now

not all poems have to be magnificent
some are just realizations
like how soap is actually important
or how you impact the world's water intake

everything to me is poetry
and as a poet i feel selfish
like my realization of how to wash dishes
actually means something.

enough to put it on paper, but it does
to realize is the arrival of creative ingestion

malnutrition, in my world of contact.
closer relations with a cutting board
i've washed six times today

than my italian neighbour
who watches the streets all day

i smile as i walk by
and from a distance sometimes i wave
but six encounters with this cutting board
turns my hands to prunes

skin shrivels around my nails, painted black
this is the first time in my life
where they're not bitten to the bone.

not all poems have to be magnificent
in fact they never should be

dreaming awake at night

you can be alive in your dreams
and crash instead of wake up

i wont exist until i find a way
to come back to myself.

i don't live here anymore
i'm in another land
on a ship soaring to morph the lines

it's what it's meant to be
but not what i want.

it's a mouth bitten mind
that's only quiet, travelling time

it's easier to be asleep
than to hear the screech with no teeth

that chews on my raw forehead
until i put it to sleep, again

it's not what it's meant to be
i know, but if i have to die with it
that's something i have to do

the silence can be life or death
and i don't know where i'm headed

patience

we watch as if
we keep our eyes steady
the bus will come faster.
winters sun speaks loud
in the eyes; we squint
and watch the corner
wait for him to make the turn
by the coffee shop
what if we knew
he would only come
once we close our eyes

intimate fluke

i apologize in advance
that i won't be there
when you wake up

you asked me to spend the night
but i'd prefer to shower at home
already forgotten who i've known

i'm sorry i'd prefer
if you could buy me a few drinks
turn this to a cinch
to pretend i'm not starved

fill my tummy until it's carved
out wrong connections

if you'd tighten on my wrists
feet would curl until they twist
up these intentions

plastic nails on your chest
subtle lines driven to divest
devours the retention
in my heart

i love how it feels.
the sensations of your flinch

form potent abrasions
where i can linger
while my body flees

so i will bite down on your lips
peel back the smallest release
binge in skin
until it brings out the crook in me

confessing there is no love
where we want it to be

backroads to paradise

tucked in the backroads
a small shop attached to the home
of a balinese tattoo artist.
i sat on a bench
drinking a bintang for breakfast.
watching fish in a tank.
as my friend lays on her hip,
her hand holds her head up
and presses into her right cheek.
a gentle grin, reveals her dimples.
her calf fills with ink
as she inhales a knockoff marlboro;
smoke formed movement
with reggaes melody
as if it spoke softly
"this is a message to you."
she asked them to take her to nirvana
and they did. they let her in the car
and drove too far
but nirvana is what you make of it.
and when you create the definition
you state it. the fish saw it too
they wondered what heaven was
as they watched her kiss filters
goodbye, in morning light.
they saw serenity
in the midst of the clouds
if only they knew
they weren't born for flight.
to embody your own meaning
is the awakening of paradise

mistfit sunrise

i've known a lot of sunrises
shaken hands with many clouds
breakfast consists of
double jack colas
and goofy bongs.
joints take hours to roll
as fingers disconnect
given themselves a name
along with the vertebrates limp
and eyes crossing games.
i make my bed every morning
before i go to sleep
stare myself down in the mirror
and watch myself creep
closer, as i stand still
she is coming for me
the woman with lost vision
and a chemical epiphany

crooked rhythm

my head
plays a song on repeat.
one i don't want to listen to
but the rhythm gives me groove
a momentum
i can't predict to you,
how it shaped the world
i thought i knew.
an ache, i can't lose
or one i don't quite want to.
it's the closest thing i have
to dancing with the blues.
i want to shake so bad
the habit
the rotation.
in an empty land
thoughts created nations.
given themselves vitality
a sense of morality
in the middle of the storm
they handcrafted

cloud nine

you learn different forms of definition
when you expose yourself

violets turn to hurricanes
clouds haven't been like this before
they've become a six on a good day

it doesn't rain; but
the thunder has a mind of its own
it's electricity stings the teeth
trembling when nerves go tense

asking for more than they deserve
it kind of makes sense;
if you distort nirvana's definition
you go crooked

i've never been like this before
rigged of definition;
where i thought it would be mended
was the centre of division

i traded soul for the hardcover
knowing too well
that was always the second reason

when you expose yourself
words turn to paint
eyes widen and swell

bodies turn into calligraphy
hearts are broken
poems are written
the detachment is quiet

lonely in a way you want it to be
because there will be no masterpiece
if the six begins to flip

repeated days

there's ash everywhere
in this house
on the rugs
in cushions
on magazines

in bedside tables
candles and plants
in every empty cup
and in full cans
of flat sodas

there's ash on
cutting boards
in the kitchen sink
ash near body wash
and where i used to think

sometimes there's ash on my cat
but she's gotten used to the smell

there's ash on wet paintings
and on thistle silk sheets
on black jumpers
and cracked concrete

there's ash in hallways
and doorways
but never the streets
ash in ash trays
with little flowers on it

there's ash in the grass
there's ash where we pray
there's ash all masked
in repeated days

ash knows better
than to flee the house
out thinking
the dependent mind

sweet tooth

i hate when i have to write
love poems.

i think of how his hands leave zest
on my spine near my hip
the way my words pare
like they're in grapefruit peels
wedged in his teeth.

he's orange juice
after my nightly ritual.

i ask the universe
why she took the tongues aspirations
she tells me to munch on lemons.
to elevate seeds and diminish fruit

all these crumpled pages
in the jarrah fruit bowl, squish
into the apples and spliff butts

even flies begin to wish
they could trace the reverie

he would write poems for me
but leave them in the crisper drawer
with week old aubergines.

when i was a kid
i would pretend to be in love,
i thought that was the start to great poets

i'd disassemble passionfruit
tap at the rind until sugar oozed
interpret it like i didn't know
i had indulged to produce cavities

i hate when i have to write
love poems.

my teeth decay and lips are gooey
before they obtain a taste
of a sucked dry cherry pit

now i see why i've adapted to limes
to distract from the hopeless theory

that poet's have a vigorous desire
to taste the sugar of an aubergine

maverick tempos

the rain welcomes
the morning.
open arms
for deep slumber,
told it's children
"this is a day of rest
please reflect
on where you pour."
there are rivers who
ache for movement
colours
that crave flux
nothing is simply still
so let's not start with us.
in the morning
god spoke to me
this is not a day,
for it's a symphony.
so in the ivory duvet
change the tempo
in which you dream
for i would never ask
that you wait for me

mind into item

every day we choose a direction to reach
so i ask harmony if she will accompany me

i ask that i continue to hover
over this ground i dance in and out of

it's a choice to steady your feet
when one step takes you away

but only for me
this path was made to run

and as i sit still my body desires
that the sober days are done

it feels as if the loss is where i've won
a shrivelled mind turned into an item

and for once i had something to hold
that tightly held me back

for once i'm meant to be somewhere
even if its in a dark room, with a potters wheel

with my head placed perfectly centred
spinning round and round to my limp touch

false awakening

this city is my coffee shop
i wish it was a little quieter
not in sound
but in profound
repetitive motions lined up.
this bus is my bench
where i sit and watch
swift forms of notion in a hurry;
these strangers
in digital fences
awaken with espresso
alive
with dull epiphanies.
this city is my coffee shop
not his or her or theirs
they have their own theory
where we don't bunch to pairs.
my coffee cup disposes
into the plastic bins
but some on the sidewalks
dance in the wind
and compose their own songs
like our feet do
on this concrete.
tapping noises
when feet glide backwards
disguise themselves in a path
as if it's not dread.
but there's a man up there
with a needle in his hand
and he winds up thin thread.
did you know?
this city is my coffee shop
not his or hers or gods
it's simply sewn together
from a desire to disconnect
and reselect
something much brighter

purple hardcover

words don't make sense
in that i've formed a collision
who knew to stay quiet
is a strange form of addiction.
to overcrowd the process of growth
by habit, or desire.
combinations of vibrations
trickle through my body
linger the longest in the brain
as if i never even saw me.
i don't say enough
or say too much
it's criminal to disconnect
from literary lust.
words scatter
i pick patterns
that dent the world i knew.
so i could shrivel up
for the hardcover
maybe it will have a golden label.
then the intentions could commence
some sort of stability
on what words represent
and why they stick to me

the messenger

i will wake up in my sleep
trying to write a landscape
lay out the format
when the poems
give no precision to me.
they are their own
i am the messenger
delivering consequences.
i am only the poet
i am only the woman
who believes
so much more than we see.
they were sent to me
and lent
to the surface of paper.
this act comes with withdrawals
of lending the woman out first
the poet is a fool
that never reaches the ground.
so this pretty woman is told
the route to the astound
they say in the paths
there will be formats
take them.
disassemble them.
ruin them.
then befriend them;
in patterns
that make us uneasy

chirping thoughts

the birds
those little bastards
they pity me.
shout through
my bedroom window.
they call me cruel names
see me in four walls
and ask where my wings are.
did i snip them on purpose
did they get caught
in heavens door?
they ask me silly questions
as if i were the one to know.
they see my room
full of feathers
and my head grown big.
the birds
those little bastards
they never shut up.
they sit on the grape vines
and beg me to get up.
i can't decline
i just nod my head
until they chirp so loud
i fall back asleep

exist nowhere

every time
i get within reach
the rain sits
under my nails
my hands flood
my body stained
the flow persists
to leak right through me.
perhaps
if i wasn't made of cotton
perhaps
if i wasn't made so porous.
what if i was crafted
in the mind
and allowed my heart to drain.
each time i get within reach
the next moment is as far
as it's ever been.
so for a while i kept my hands
in my pockets
and only took them out
for the summer sand.
that's why moments like this
frighten me.
the ones where i
sit unwilling
to open my hands.
yet still, it all rushes past

abstract woman

i, bone abstraction
of inner earth
external in flesh
i, expression of the ocean
mountains and stars.
a facile painting.
a result of the storm.
i, the utterance
quieted in speech
roars in vitalities preach
i, a form of fruit
of gods, of branches
sweetness
like orange peels
taking reigns from
whiskeys pungent edge.
though we still cherish
the bare entity
in abrupt tangy notes
i, an abundance
of untold truth
weep in depths
for movement
i, vibrations
turn to nerves
encounter raw form
from eager lust
to tender love.
all touch is vulnerable
organic and pure
when it's titled to be
the body

saint with horns

angels manifest dusty pages
shape shift into epiphanies
with two horns.
known results in the dark
while i hide the light.
don't you know
down below
humans are so giddy
with big frowns
jewelled crowns
eating soggy hearts
of the city.
digging for a muse
in muddled beliefs
of monarchs.
apologizes to the angels
for fiddling with their scraps
as they manifest
an achy soul
and cruising body
who accuses the wrong woman.
don't point fingers
away from your mind
put your hands on your knees
welcome two horns
knowing the white wings
will come when
immorality surrenders

no love

black and purple bones
on the spine
from the bathtub
that drains too quickly.
faster
than it ever cares to fill.
drill holes in the brain
the arms, the cunt, the touch.
bruises
are poor losers
always asking
for too much.
moldy minds bloat
with the stomach
looking for news to shout
from the penthouse.
silence shrivels with my vision
the only words detected,
and barely mumbled
"i said my final goodbyes
yet here i am again."
the stars are louder
prouder
than gunpowder
in the eye of the enemy.
no fuss over the abuse
just no more blood
i beg
it's a whore out for prey
down on two knees
calling on the creator

night owns us

the night owes us nothing
only to collide as we offer our breath

in the midst of the dark our feet lose reach
so we raise our arms and voices until we float

offering dances of our muse
deep infused in our hands

we follow rhythm like it's god
when the night only asked to realize
we aren't mimickers of impulse

we lend our mind out
so the soul has reference

this is an expression
of how the poet persist
to demand fancy with the night

like how the clouds shy past the moon
with no resistance in the flux

the night owes us nothing
as long as we understand
how foolish it would be to ask

which world is this

twiddle fingers
shake shake
lack pattern
lack persistence
unless anonymous
twiddle fingers
shake knees
talk to bees
lose concentration
on the clouds
lost in the complex
mind of no subject
shake
race
trace the letters
aching tease
repetition of please
make tomorrow vary
twiddle fingers
shake
ache
my spine gathers
the brain's pain
awake, shake
does the bend
break
twiddle fingers
uncontrolled

pity paradox

crash deep
but subtle
like tequila
in coffee
to ease the
word puddle.
heighten expression
rolled up discretions
burned slowly.
together
we've worn down
is this what we
wanted?
exactly.
the sensation
never could
have been predicted
although as a child
i was addicted
to the concept
of deterioration
what an uneasy
feeling, to know
i thrived for this

blood or honey

bind to nothing
except where i wont go
the body is earth in a frame, mine
consumed
by the blood of grapes

past lives pretend to live on
bounce off the skull
imitate the voices.
a dull preach demands
to expand for the sacred pages

let loose to learn grip.
so my body turns to yarn
i am tied to each pillar of sin
creating a web of false intimacy

i wish love had another killer
but time knows it's way around the blade

and when blood ran low
it was eagerly replaced.

still in the shade of maroon
and in the texture of cold honey
dripping to the soil

i thought it was sweet syrup
because i was stuck to the floors
but when i looked up at heaven
the ashes of it poured

the closest i've ever been to love
i stood under realities door
locked behind wide eyes
searching and searching
unsure
of what i was searching for

solace in purgatory

absences stock up
in black leather boots
deterioration
starts at the root.
glitch steps, laced up
rising heartbeat to the
dismissal of prayers.
beg to break even
but never ask.
where's the purity
in this lucid grin
when i've been
in the centre of anarchy;
during foul cries.
absent thoughts
cherries rot in the centre
of a plastic bag.
sweetness wasted
stifled
in a counterfeit haven.
perished sugar
passes purgatory
on its way down
astound
by the presence
held in refusal.
savoury
touches the surface
until you dig your teeth
in over ripe peaches
break one. break two
slice your tongue on the pit
sentences spill out
ooze from your mouth
with insentient
the overdue
of nirvanas echo
staggers the mind.
imploring
to be baptized
by unholy waters

god's way

the stars are above my head
green and chemical pressed
into a spliff and tucked
between my teeth.
i feel a sense of life.
i ask the gods questions
and i know
i know i got answers
i'm not sure what they are
but i don't need to.
the stars start conversations
talk in ways that make me think
i'm talking to myself.
not only inspiring my thoughts
but become them.
crawl into my fingers
remind me
i'm not fully dead yet
inhale, a switch of perception
i think this is the god's way
of connection.
we all have our own
type of spiritual

letter to myself

the unseen truth
is that i miss you dearly.
i apologize for burying you
beneath gods nightmares

i've had epiphanies
in overcrowded pleasures.
i've spoiled our bones
and traded our flesh

i found, there's no treasure
when nirvanas extended.
and that love in the night
sleeps through the days

i have missed you sincerely
yet i'm not sure who you are.
i forced upon the poet
now the woman takes the blame

aching to be everywhere at once
but i'm in the walls of my head
writing letters to a stranger
in hope she's on the other end

is this to the young girl
or the shape shifting woman
i'm not sure which one i am
i'm not sure which one is talking

i got a letter back with no name
it said the dreams were not as dark
there were times she got to heaven
'tho still restless, it was pure

she said "i am here.
even in the mornings.
so for now, you can be my dreams
in the never-ending night."

repercussions

repercussions
where do they come in
at the crack of dawn
or fissure of relations

detach to rewire
artificially posed sensations

a daze infused with a sense of faith
dictate time in darkness
lightening white lights
the ceasing entity mimics grace

oaths devoured by dependency
bent vows, paid dues.
all morality let loose

dissecting the passion of growth
that now wilts to distress.

we sold a fraud of self definition
for overbearing white
lies, beneath clammy skin

the angel of earth aches to surrender
but there's no mercy for the wicked.
only elegance in the show
on stage, read a page
and then would they know?

i reckon not, up in their head
interior viewpoint knots
jumble up the veracity.

repercussions
damned to discussions
with only the cat, lighter and spliff

mutter life into sequences
never known better

than to muzzle weakness
and kill the witness

repercussions
overthrown by the dialect
in me, there are more of us

disassembled unity rearranges impulses
in a way that does not guarantee life.

seek for results in unresolved places
seek for impacts of recurring
mangle of mind, of body.

slowly it disperses over sticky grounds
latches to the souls, of the feet

repercussions
have rotated with delicacy
spin, between the eyes
ever so discreetly

dizzy wisdom
reciprocates unconscious love
delivered by the poet
resulting in a finicky hand
and lonely mornings

wilted nerve

we've got apricots in the fridge
a few mangos and golden kiwis
next to the curdled yogurt
and blue bread.
the banana tree in the backyard wilts
the fruit reaches for overgrown grass
and stretches it's arms for me.
my hands, unable to be lent
they were slower than the rain
in the summer.
down the city lane
in the old brick house
i'd wait inside for the drops
to show their rhythm
on the windows glass
quietly sit still in no silence
as i sit on my bed
the grapes bloom and shrivel
scared i'd drink their juice.
as the figs weep
erupt in their own skin
will their tears do us good
i will wait and see
behind this window

unknown offerings

open your mouth
tighten permission
in each form except pages.
soak up spilt love with a cloth.

open your mouth
don't let them see
light a candle
make me wash my sheets
don't stay the night
if you do, leave early

open your mouth
until your lips foam with courtesy.
become vulnerable to my barricades
and don't appear loving in lust

open your mouth
reach out your hand, offer me a glass
that seeps of the classified
spill out sweet nothings
for me to get drunk on

open your mouth
tingle my tongue
don't kiss me though
it resembles love

legs widen, tighten of abdomen
i give you permission, to tread the surface
hail an abundance of absence

open your mouth
wring the cloth out
the chalice is out of reach
let it stay there
adjure the drops, cherish them

i've already been generous
to only cry at gods feet

half a poet

half a poem
wiggles the spell
of fire burning the reckless.
respect the wish of the writer
to become better out of absence.
evolution
out of numb tension
is the intention of a fool
who pretends
she never hid
with hands full of fuel.
lost grip, move with
an unintended scurry
out of time, lost clocks
a distant mother
nurtures worry.
half poems represent well
what the mind portrays.
like a portrait of the process
still. in ridden waves.
half a poem
sits on the edge of patience.
rolled up, await the spark
invite colour from congestion.
wait for walls to turn to foam
soft. posh script
and muse of stone.
half a poem
sinks into seven a.m. coffee
when the mug is
half empty
or full.

split messages

the only time
my mind is blank
is when the page
coordinates with it
maybe its a form of prayer
while i wait for poetry
to recite itself
telling me
the pattern
of withering emotions
offering structure
to an impulsive spew.
only the chosen knew
the direction
we were headed.
at eight years old
i knocked my head in
with a wine glass, white
words found
a crevasse to reside
until they dripped red
and i indulged
deeper than they asked.
i blame it on the first sip
that split me in two
running blue, yellow
and red, seduce temptations
uncivil creation
from a never blank mind

poet's prospect

artist devoured by desperation
darts morph to drops of wine
drip from the chalice
punctures flesh.

lips ooze, eyes burn.
let not the skin rot, just loosen;
while the mind refuses orders

artistic desolation
only exists in tangible jungles
the insides must roar
with shut eyes and sharp teeth

take a glimpse around
but know not when to sleep
forbidden hours are most awake
when the mind devours
shoulders ache

legs twitch
the honeypots empty and drips
clean up the mess we've made
be vulgar with your kiss
draw blood in circles.
love only what you miss.

devoured by desperation
let it howl. to assume silence
is to poke the eyes of the poet
then let the red ooze
into an uncanny resemblance
of death

get close. and run your fingers
through my dress. maybe then
i'd gain a little passion
so the poet can confess
it's daring troubles

tender comfort

morning have mercy
for the prospect is muddled
building its own passion
gathering it's own face
poise in posture
bathed in purple.
asking at each sun
to be brought back again.
minimal composure
begs for misplacement
of grace, eyes linger
mouth loosens
voice imitates
cigarettes.
morning coffee
desired awakening
a glimpse of
orders taste.
what a waste, an
empty mug
jumble up words
scramble, for love
found in grains
like a cherished
polaroid picture
in an opaque frame.
pause prosperity
patient sincerity,
becomes fretful
morning have mercy
for i lost love.
i lost words and
definitions of above.
lets cheers our glasses
to those we speak of.
and to no humility
in the house of the poet

unreached

tears drip
from versace glasses
wallow
in the sun's pity.
fall through
the drivers window
to twinkle
in the passing river.
eyes fixated
and stiff
debunk the theory
that love didn't count
cause we were drunk
most the time.
blinked
into a paradox
lust or
consumption
but not love.
unless it was stuffed
in an unwilling box
with a brief introduction
of organic wine
and windy sunsets
carrying my words
past him

sudden split

quick
we move quick
quick
delinquents trace
signs of a rush
rushing to be quick
to dive into an act
of a demure
but i am sure
i'll get rundown
quick
but do it slick
sensual groove
has nothing to prove
when it's woven
in the anarchies womb
stretching new skins
until new life breaks in
to tarnish intimacy.
rushes
of slaps of blues
of you
you
you ruined it all.
it was me.
i apologize
but only to myself

abstract painting

the purple carousel
never stop spinning
it stirs consistent agony
with only a drop of passion

dissect all blues with a fraud
of innocent distraction
that possesses love
by running far
in circles

in sparse flees, we become.
in the comas there's no light

the inability to control what's done
is fragile, in steady form
waiting to be worn
down by capricious love

riding the back of brief consumption
drunk and bare to the bone
in the middle of daytime streets

everything i've ever felt
is in the trunk of the car
when we keep driving

or the box under the stairs
where we pretend it's grey

repetitive visits
each morning
and each night
he's blue in my dreams
but red comes for a fight

provokes vulnerability in a glass
last couple sips pour it out
to the dispersed desire
at last

restless hunger

i can't sleep.
i move the blankets in funny ways
silk, fleece, and a cloud like duvet
legs plopped over, aligned with my waist
arms above my head
or fingers move to taste myself.
enlighten the nerves
twice.
i still can't sleep
i think of you briefly
but i'd rather get off to
the thought of my managers hands
reaching up my dress in his office.
cause when i think of you
i think of how i'd tell you off
and it ruins the mood.
the window is open
persuading the room
to match the outdoor breeze
even in this soothing air
i still cannot sleep.
my body won't loosen
my brain won't groove
into censorship, just left to right
tighten in the ears
they ring, sting my thoughts
with tension as if i needed more.
ideas stretched out of my head
what i need is a moment of silence
let's pour one out
for the death of impressions
that you buried
and i kept digging up.
i just cannot sleep
and if i could
i still couldn't
resist the dreams
drawn in at the seams
of the alarm clock, shouting
that you're sleeping like a baby
with or without me

crying from below

wilted eyes
shapeless vision
fingers adjust the next tunnel.
another journey
to keep god hidden
my eyes can't water
when i'm on the other side
just dissipate into a thought.
the joint is now rolled
i haul on it   slowly
it keeps me company
in a way
that writes its own story.
accompany the jitters
with more jitters
jitters with context
jitters with purpose
these jitters
don't take time
to discover.
jitters
that flinch the core
and expand fingers.
wilted eye, avoid
eye contact with myself
as it's much too intimate
to see a glimpse
of refrained weeping

a long way from home

touch my waist
but not my spine
race your fingers
to lingerie strings
play with the edges.
kiss my neck deeply
my lips only briefly
kiss my legs
and look at me.
pull the black lace
towards you
make your way
between me
you'll see my eyes soften
as i feel your tongue eagerly.
praise me in this moment
make me yours
in this moment
there won't be coffee
or more wine
or a god to pray to
in the morning

mama

mama tells me my eyes droop with the blues
mama tells me they're red
and the boys i live with are bad news

mama tells me she wants me back home
mama tells me she's proud
but the cries are too loud to pretend

mama tells me the feelings of her hugs
while my past two years have been
swept beneath the rugs

mama tells me i should quit smoking
my voice is raspy and skin is soaking
in ash puddles. that's all she knows.

mama said wait until i was twenty-one
when i was six-teen, but i won.
losers are not meant to be sacred

mama sends me scripture verses
and i cry sometimes if i read them
so i try to just delete them

sometimes mayhem is welcomed
and sometimes mama would be proud

nineteen forty two

he closes his eyes around me
the radiance swallows me raw.
don't talk. if we know less
we can't pick love.
buy me two,
make me cocktails
with nineteen forty two
back with the apartment views.
the river makes the city
seem empty at night
as i overlook
i feel myself spill
over the balcony
of the eighteen floor.
we sit quietly with tequila.
i stroke my nails
through his overgrown hair.
in the mornings
i lie awake, naked.
trace my fingers
over the tattoo
on the back of his shoulder.
and when he wakes up
in the afternoon
he showers alone
and drives me home

tantalize

can we sit here a moment?
light cigarettes backwards
watch the flame
like an antidote
of what we consumed
so harshly.
in each pour we have
tantalized
any meaning behind it
to distract from
how the origin diverted.
and as inspiration
trickles down my throat
my face stays steady
sometimes
i close my eyes
for a brief moment
and i know why it began.
an addiction
with a purpose.
except pages stayed empty
or crumpled by tension
shifted into behaviour.
lets light it once
from the edge
and kiss down on the filter
suffocate its delicacy
and then you'll know
you've stilled her.
withdrawn her
from the body
digging deeper
digging deeper.
she ate bitter ends
left many loose
got close to the amends
but always chose the bitter youth.
bloody cuticles
and burnt stomach
lighting cigarettes
and burning homes

hocus pocus

out of focus
hocus pocus
erosion with an aim
remove the body
diddily daddly
puts daring tendencies
into a frame.
hey you sir
i've seemed to forgot
what to blame.
what's your desires
and deepest shame?
out of focus
what's the bonus
when you slur your words
every night.
we haven't got
a name in the day
and we lost it again
at night. out of focus
let's lose our minds
in the epiphany of
destruction.
suck words
from the poet
twice. soak my brain
in rice, in a plastic bag
in a fire escape
in a loose pocket
or a crack
in the sidewalk

wake up call

i woke up
and the time was the same
as when i fell asleep
four thirty five a.m.
my eyes were closed
but days froze
with the feeling
of his silent commands.
i closed my eyes
but i didn't dream.
the clouds filled my nerves
until i could see clearly
white stars.
the scars, rotate.
would he ever know
when my eyes close
if his always close first.
watch the ceiling too often
after i shake his shoulders
cold. bold in loss of intimacy
kisses are criminal
before midnight
i woke up
and the time was the same
as when i was frightened
by my own shape
rigged of most my years
for the submission
to the impulse.
banging my nail
into the ceiling
interferes with the dreams
that linger
when i'm half awake

shatter in depths

my body of glass
shatters on the demon's front lawn.
two horns are crooked lines
on a head pleading
out wiggling cries

but they lie, they do
to shoo their truth away.
into fingertips that grip to lips
to hide what they might pray

do we know anyone at all
what if we untied the braids
connecting our walls.

protect the centre of impaled desires
don't push too deep
or you'd move the inquire
to the spoiled gut

rot in the wobble of it all
foundation of mirrors, oh sweet dear
where did you go? do we owe
the royalty our tears?

where's the love they deserve
for feeding the hungry youth

we've offered years to dust
that falls off intentions
to reconcile with the lost mind
keepings scraps of a love never known

suspend the heart from the game
extends the darts, aimed
for the wicked.

lands in eyes
that looks through peepholes
trying to see the future

we found freedom
in loss of control.

do we know, do we know
do we know they took it from us
the impulse dismantled
our view of self unity

and now we lift our chins
in the middle of the battle.
close our eyes and breathe in
confessing that sin
doesn't have a definition

stragglers faith

my car has been running
off desperation sent to god
good riddance to the facade
of the naive children in me

a letter sealed between palms
and wilted by dusk.

days only carry envelopes
through early air.
the pen only draws
in the hopeless choir

lose myself
for a moment
while i drive too fast
for a moment.
do the ones next to me notice
what god has done to me

they'd never know
and i could only pray
they find out.

it's not my devotion
to negotiate the rotation given
by who i named god.

i skid the surface of the road
press the gas, move too fast
until the ride drives itself.

we lost faith
except we never fully did

even in the hysterical abrasion
of the child. hands folded together
in the middle of the facade

putrid purpose

cherries pop
over the single gash on my chest
a crease looks for a sugar rush

drizzle sticky residue in cue
with the leaking tongue

oozing booze into good news
wiggles an uncanny resemblance
of tampered love.

my head dances off my neck
rolls, for the crows

they'll sit in rows and wait for me
to turn to vinegar jam

latch to the edge of the blade
pressed flat into burnt rye bread

honey bones

bones made of honey
taste skins edge
sink into desires
to turn me blue.
lack of air
can't we share
some pleasure;
treasures
of the damned
wrapped in capsules
bottles, tongues and tingles
between legs.
stick to desperation.
stick to my golden heart.
don't ever wonder, where
i've been without you.
loosen discretion
like i've hit freshly made tea.
a woman of honey
you can taste but can't touch
is it too much to ask
to reframe my lust.
let my mind dissolve
into the bodies rapture.
bones made of honey
won't you come with me tonight
as we stroll down the coastline
make a home on the edge.
take our clothes off in the cold
and share a bottle of wine
anything to make me feel
as if i have dissolved
into the rhymes of
the lonely poet

lovers new lover

rum on rocks
squished lime
pure sublime
until the grief hit.
spit my mouth out
it doesn't belong in tears.
i cherish it, in a way
as it's the only time i sway
back and forth by nerves
instead of force of thought.
try not to rot
just cry in the taxi home.
it won't dress tomorrow
it'll impress marijuana
as we slowly spin nirvana.
it's real pain
that makes you feel
like you're not greedy
for trying to survive.
bitter thoughts
tighten the bones
and lacken strive.
i'd rather be an astronaut
with rum on the rocks,
not looking in the wild
for colour changing clocks
i'd rather be where
there is not enough room
for lovers
lack of goodbyes

sorrow's limbo

i don't go to sleep
because i'm tired
anymore.
satin tightens at my skin
for the sake of relieved sin.
dispersed
into the dead of sleep.
we won't weep
between comfort
only beg for mercy
in the morning.
with legs crossed
and hands intertwined.
where will we find
the divine
in time.
i haven't been able
to seek for it
when i do,
tables wobble and
under eyes turn blue.
night used to be
my favourite of hours
devouring
lost intentions of day.
let loose
like drops of vermouth
in a lemon twist martini.
who wins?
in the never ending game
of push and pull

the endless race

if i forgot to mention
i'm on ecstasy
but does it really matter
it's the best of me
smoothed lines
always too thick
but there's no such thing
in a world like this
stacked bottles
narcotics in cracks
each crease is an interstice
to a new universe
the world is ours
they just don't know it yet
we drove the fastest
and tried to believe
we would make it home

falling up

what part of it do you see
cause i've disassembled internally

eyes closed, mouths expression
battles between snarling and a grin.

even if a tear could catch my lips
the tongue chases anything to quiet the leak.

reaching for another glass
the last was in the past

so i am clear headed
ruling the land of royalties fools

the feathers were white
along with the lights we searched for

when i hold my breathe
i see the stars, sometimes
they tell stories
of a way to get back home

to get out of the throne,
demanding submission to the chalice

to consume what i already am
then maybe i could become
something more

dragged for the ride

we move too fast
for this city.

in the backseat every night
i see the buildings chase me

they devour me
until i come home

fingers dance goodbye
eyes roll to the heavens

dazed in fictional stars
we know it's not true

but the city is ours

midway land

which reality is this
the one soft like butter
on a blueberry muffin.
sink into dents
and off the edge
drizzled attention
to sweet friction?
we're never where we are
until we mention
it never stops dripping
  time
in our fingers,
thoughts and toes.
smooth resistance
to stand still
as if we chose the heat.
is this the one
where i stutter for prevention
of too many words
of maybe the wrong ones.
i feel rot
introduce itself to the heart
shake hands, as if it's got
something nice to say.
is this the reality where
the berries heat up
distorted sugar
erupting from suffocation.
the crows are hungry
for our sickness
in search for bloated bellies.
there is never enough words
to describe this blissful
weakness

cracked detail

the middle shelf is busted
it always falls back
where you can't see.
disturbs the top
blocks the bottom drawer
rattles the bukowski
and watts books above
by the jarrah fruit bowl
full of old smokes
dirty socks
car keys
and seashells.
the damned middle shelf
fucked up any wholeness left
in this spider filled van,
like a thief who steals
love from the lonely

solitary reset

bruised and cut noses
are losers, to the end game
shift their shade
their marvel. in stillness
eyes are further than here

deep in green forests
or picking up pieces
left from a lover.
in bed i lay again, alone.
at least this way the silk sheets
can hang off the edge in peace

blankets don't need covers
mornings need more sleep.
i could wake up, if i wanted
but i'll snooze until four hours past
my six a.m. alarm clock

beep, beep, beep
it doesn't even make that noise.
the word rattles in my head
reminding me no ones around
to wake me up anymore

and i'd open eyes for sunrise
drink coffee in a yellow and red mug
with apple and grape vines wrapping it
they'd spin around my fingers
and keep me warm in the early frigid

gradual apricity appears
only in the ear, rings like a church bell
come back to me
come back to me
god will ask, and i'll agree

but then i'll sit there lonely
jealous of my coffee
for having the company of oat milk

friend of the devil

i never danced with the devil
i gave him my hand
and he told me to be still.
absorb the killers thrill
take the pill
allow it to move for you
consume for you
target hearts in parts, detach
them from the blues.
move with me, he said
we will go far, see canopies
with christmas lights, in the sky.
we'll celebrate everyday
the death of christ, in you
and you'll see everything
outside of your body
it'll be textured like
blood coloured play-doh
stain the hands, act as glue
in the prayers. never stop
you don't deserve to

in the jungle

the universe
won't let you outthink it.
you have to be submissive
to dissolve true desires.
you'll lose faith
if you keep looking
for everything you have.
it's a story either way.
you can't punish crime
but you'll get lost in it.
do time, make it a rhyme
become a slave to the jungle
on the run, without your head.
you ate it.
so you wouldn't see
what you'd become.
the jungle has a mind of its own
to chew up resistance
then spit it out
to build the egos throne.
i still pity the queen
who will never love
like i can
and as i mock her
i sleep on the floors
of her temple.
i'll follow her silly rules
and offer myself
to her gentle smother
that holds a sweet smell
of retained freedom

gradual latch

i was sober all day
then my brother couldn't stay
so i smoked a joint in the field.
my mum said don't smoke dope
in the pastor's friend's yard
but then i'd never smoke
in the suburbs.
i'm alone right now
so i need the company
stuffed in a cylinder
spread through me
like waves of small kisses
from a loved one i've outgrown.
my lover is my heart,
who's never been loyal.
i sit there in the morning
at the breakfast table
and it passes by me
it passes by me
and it passes by you
what day is it now
drinking coffee alone
cause my lover is sleeping in
for the fourteenth time
this week

retained ex lover

looking through a pile of clothes
when everything you own is black
is no fun.
cleaning alcohol off leather heels
with makeup remover and a tea towel
is no fun.
small talk
burnt toast
curdled milk
seeing ghosts
is no fun.
drinking a fly who died in wine
and seeing it as a sign, is no fun.
it's like stale cookies
sour tofu
itchy muzzles
out of tune radios
wet books
good looking crooks
bent in hooks
they're no fun.
unreciprocated love
loose wires
and unheated homes
in the winter, are no fun.
uncollected gifts
drunken night shifts
fuckable managers
those are only fun
for the ego.
lingering eyes
misplaced triggers
and using jiggers
are no fun
uneducated doctors
unfolded laundry
undesired touches
and wine corked a month ago
are no fun
burnt tongues

from morning tea
broken condoms and
men who want to sleep over
are no fun
smirnoff shots
burnt out batteries
damp socks
and jammed locks
they all provide
the same feeling
of leaving the house
of a retained ex lover
at night
for the very first time

dear young woman

i don't know what's worse
a jump from your own reflection

or heart drop from your shadow.
is it the details or outline?

is it shivers when you see bloodshot eyes
or seeing the body swollen

from the emotional corpse
rotting with desire to come back to life.

fragments of cut lips, dirty clothes, raspy voice
but a lustful smile and thin rhythmic curve

your figure is what they can pry on
encourage a taste, seasoned with flirtatious pity

they'll help you laugh, you could surely use it
and you'll love seeing those fools go mad.

honesty is the outline, you can tease them to the edge
and they'll get nervous from their own perception.

they'll be pleased in their own eyes
remembering the woman who drinks whiskey straight

they see your smile for weeks
and you will sit there with a joint

thinking about any other man
kissing up your thighs

life in momentary death

i came here to consume revival
become a part of the wild flowers
to lay in the field
and feed myself to the bees

they'd only sting if there was fear
so they never did

i was an imposter
fostering adolescent clarity

in the forms of honey whiskey
and distant touch
joints at three a.m
and asking for too much

from the girl in four inch heels
and a four inch dress

i knew i'd never make it
if i kept shedding layers
off falsely accused access

i came here to consume revival
now death is alive
and i am the rival;

creating comfort in an
irreversible state of mind

smooth stingers introduce
a flinch in nirvana

revives the view where
the corner of death may be
the gateway
to melodious
sweetness.

playing out an irking rhythm

that slowly becomes me
i was waiting and
i was waiting

for the tempo to slow its pace
i was waiting and
i was waiting

for the voice
in a sonata

devil's lust

could you meet the devil
on tuesday's sunrise
after the downfall of heavens reprise
playing the wrong keys

could you preach the devil's
early possession
even know you'd be bruised
on four knees

could you reach the devil's
caffeinated implications
when you are handed
the pot of dandelion tea

could you steal the devil's
silly prescriptions
and forge them to be
something worse

could you, would you
let the devil make your panties wet
until you lose him in the crowd
and pay your heart the debt

could you feel the devil watch you
like you're in a tight sheer dress
your eyes glance, red lips smirk
poised in his confining possession

could you teach the devil
how you did it with elegance
how you chewed the man's ears
and still he wanted to hear
how you did it

luminary in disguise

i'll be grateful for the day
i brush my teeth
every morning and night.
the day i get to crawl into a made bed
with sheets washed every month

in the mirror i saw what it'll be.
we multiply ourselves
take the previous to choose
wiser next time

i'll keep symptoms
change behaviour.

i'll be grateful for the day
i'm given flowers, i think
i know men all wrong

my heart wrapped in wires
when my body ran to wicked love
not allowing the mind to cry.
'cause if i did
my life would run.

i'll be grateful for the day
i wake up for the sunrise
and take my dog for a walk
intertwine grass with bare feet

maybe have a coffee
where the oat milk isn't burnt

maybe read a book
about the rolling stones or
pablo neruda.
smiling at myself
for the fool i had been

self induced

new life growls in the stomach
athletic critters follow passion
knowing not their faction
slivering to the heart
swell up
with sugar and bad news
like ankles trying
to wear new leather shoes
in the summer.
my naval cradles up to me
acts as if it fancies my spine
a cleanse for the gut
marijuana
triple espresso
now what
if i am not shrinking
where am i going?
am i on route to the dependents
running
every time i reach my head.
or sulking in my sorrows
and taking them to bed.
new life grows
in unforeseen places
traces the waist
of a young woman
brutally coughing up pieces.
the muse is in the fourth glass
the leach is in the fifth
the writer rules its parade
by the tenth.
and in the mornings
hearts will growl
minds will snarl
and hair has its own thoughts
the sneaky poet
tied my assumption
to the top of the ceiling
with a latch to insert my wrists

the awaited surrender

i stood in my bedroom
with the lights off
in an ivory lace bra
my hair knotted
and eyes drowsy.
i began to dance
my cat sat across from me
and did not look away.
the moon was the only light
and it shun bright
into tears
slipping down
closed eyes.
the cat never looked away
and when a single tear
hit the ground
i dropped to my knees
and put my paws
in front of hers.
she was a skittish cat
but she did not flinch.
so i stood.
i slowed with the music
allowed the tears
to fill me, for the first time
in over a year.
i turned on the lamp
looked into the copper eyes
of that boney fostered cat.
i kneeled,
she slowly stood
walked to me
and rested on my lap

burning relief

i strike a match
and it sparks the feeling of you
i light the end of a cigarette
your kiss
it's the closest thing to.

i wish i'd lose my need for you
but i strike all these matches
and roll up little pieces of you

if i could look you in the eye
the hazel would see me through
i wish i could've said goodbye
even when i didn't need to

i let the match burn to my fingers
i let the sun rotate without me
i let myself think i loved you
for i was too afraid
to belong to me.

pretty woman

i'm a pretty woman
with her legs spread
on the footrest
slouched shoulders
pressed into cushions
… eyes droopy
a thinned out bun
and frayed hairs
… shrivelled voice
never enough weed
and caffeine
for her tiny frame.
swollen from past lives
as she sits quietly
to soak up death.
praying to be reborn
in the vessel of a poet
… they say
i'm a pretty woman
and of course
that's what they know
she never loved them
but her sister knows,
her ex lovers know
and surely god too
… heels play games
dresses are teasers
she is a woman
who can outdrink any man
as long as he knows
what day it is.
always asking for more
and never for permission.
… the composition of her love
is in snarky glances
midnight stargazes
eyes on your back
and joints pre rolled.
… i'm a pretty woman
they tell me

in her four inch heels
and her four inch dress
with fourteen tequila shots
keeping her on route
to find her own head
but the road splits to four
and the hills turned red
so she rode the incline
smoking a spliff
out the car window
listening to a combination
of mötley crüe and bob dylan

distanced

don't love your lover
don't get them drunk and extend laughter

don't remove yourself from the dirt
as if sprouting seeds is an evil plan

i do think it's hopeless
biting a mans tongue

i could chew it and spit it out
before they'd know

they bloat from tendencies to absorb
misconstructed tattle tales

read by an old man
who lost his eyeglass

don't love your lover
they might just love you too

sticky rising

if you notice the small things
parts of it would collide
in slow conclusions.
that there's blood
surfacing on arms
mouth and fingers.
finally the nails have grown
but the lips are now swollen
like a bee mistook me
for a field of wild flowers.
my pinky nail near to the bone
skin peeled
like i'm picking off peddles
for a desired lover.
it takes too much time
to loosen my shoulders.
if you notice the small things
you would see a battle
between a child
and the heavens.
scraped knees in the climb
bruised chins, dug itself
into easels, on display.
i ask my mom to pray for me
my lungs barely know their name
then i sit there smiling
at my joint.
if you notice the small things
i wonder what you could tell me.
once you know what i am now
with little wings, a raspy voice
and eyes that have chapters
in an unpublished book.
subtly the muse turns the blues
into future paintings
believing in purples.
just this once

satiated heart

feel it in your knees
the tickling persuaded us further
moved us in directions of stillness
for once there is a silence
besides the ringing of ears
but that sticks around
day and night
as if my body craves
communication
further than words.
that are jumbled
as if scrabble was taught to toddlers
bend your knees like a lotus
become a loop of progression
suspend distance in growth
home is where the heart is
and the heart was only seeds
in the jungle. we mumble now
out of hesitation
of where the preach
could take us.
crooked speech
is a hefty crime
for a poet.
attempt to rewrite
what's been written
in hope it can satiate
the hungry heart

frequencies

the universe is a series
of vibrations.
let your body loose
dance through moments.
follow life's rhythm.
why be the static
when you can tune in

forged world

spliff lives on in the dead hand
going against the rivers pattern
continuous tremble or vibration
a call for an unknown fix.
but this is it
the middle of the storm
roots sway, currents rush
to follow the given path.
have i been here?
or did i get swept up
pondering in the rapids.
i have somewhere
urgent to go
i have no idea where.
what is this ache
this cry
this resistance.
making me small.
now my eyes see her jump
out of the moving car
just before sunrise.
so i run to see
nobody is there

rational lover

i flirt with irrational lovers
it feeds an impatient heart.
intrinsic touch
is not a familiar reach
for the one who
swallows every pill presented;
until sobrieties in a capsule.
alter, shift, resist, dissolve.
not until now have i ever
seen a rational lover in my head
not until now
have i ever seen him
wait for me to drive away
before he goes inside
or make sure i've eaten enough.
the irrational lovers
flirt with my innocence
and greedy desires
left stranded
on an island i swam to.
their names, only letters
binded into elastic hearts.
not once in my life
have i ever thought of
holding hands or candle lit dinners
it's always been
mouths silently slipping on waists
and men who claim to be winners.
the irrational lover in me
has been brought to reason
brought to dinner of a new taste
based off the way this man
still kisses me
in the mornings

twenty

three of us with soaked bathers
on the ledge, and a bottle of x.o. tequila

drunken poker players romance
in the cascades of a hotel room

foolish lust for the club owner, losing
focus while trying to free pour a drink

overload of champagne and don julio
the sex i barely remember, the fantasies i do

naked swims at the beach at midnight,
after a bottle of wine and four joints

two zen buddhism books and
a meditation room where i painted while drunk

crack of dawn is bed time, write
morphed sequences with squinted eyes

finish charles bukowski's entire collection
of the pleasures of the damned

quit two jobs, drop out of school and get on a plane
home. i was waiting there for myself

trapped in between. still leaking to the bottom
of the other side, stretching into a vanished eternity

a sunset behind the mountains and coastline, honey whiskey
and a mind that made more sense than i did

a bed in the back of a rusted suzuki, parked in a field
woken by the early sun and a kiss from my love

static

stereo head
wraps tunes
engraved
in the wicked trap.
snap my jaw in two
the never calm current
pulls me to the border
in the late night.
dropping eyes
like chips onto
a roulette table.
it's a shame
some people
have never had
a radio in their head

identity shift

i've lived in this room from two
until i was eighteen
and then again at twenty.

it's had purple walls and
flowers lining the ceiling
then everything painted black
except the white furniture.

it had beatles posters, grateful dead
and collections of stuffed animals
concert tickets, printed photos
jar-less candles and poetry books

when i was younger i liked to see what i had
now here i am and i can barely remember.
i sit and look around the room
while my dog snores on my leg.

the tapestry echoes blues
and burgundy flares mimic the sun,
behind a papasan chair.
an alan watts book and my journal
are in reach, on the wooden dresser.

two holes in the window screen
from when i was sixteen smoking darts
on the roof, with my musician boyfriend
who wore a grocery store fur coat
and black ripped jeans.

then i was twenty sitting on the roof
smoking a joint, looking
over the grey nights suburban fog
in a black thong and oversized tee.
this room feels more mine
than it ever has

anticipated split

culprits play jazz
meet at the crossroads
i out waited them all
for the eroded wall
so i could build a bookshelf.
for once it all made sense
then it didn't
then i'm torn
between the two
and now i'm ridden,
by the criminal
i've turned into.
the devil won't take the past
but the games ensure it wont last
results in a tremble calling out
for something i can't identify.
anejo, straight on ice
give me answers
don't be nice, just don't say
i should've obeyed
and just don't name the price.
anejo, please play the roll
of my inner anarchy parade.
give me grace, a gentle face
to hide the crying child in me.
each moment is frayed
before i even prayed to
the woman i might be.
i heard the blues
in abstract paintings
i heard the blues
in cruelly written poems
i heard the blues
ringings in my ears
as the walls hit the ground.
i strapped myself to the criminal
who was an eager writer.
for once it all made sense
and then it didn't
and with every pill of logic

the poet swallowed,
the woman was forbidden
from the world in front of me;
so she could build a bookshelf
made from her own brain
and a few knocked out teeth

under discovery

journals hold too much for me
i can read how the body moves
scared, curled over celebrations.
the mind moves, giggles
like death closing in
on a decayed life.
i should cry, but i don't.
stiff body, strip rhythm
until dissonance
makes a peaceful song.
if this calls for more effort
from myself, the leader
will know almost
as much as i do.
except i make the choice
to surrender the egos love
or depend on empty routines.
it feels i am carried to mud
i could be the pig
but i will be the seed.
salvations
in the burning home
and i've run in
for my missing lover
who was never found.
deep down i don't like it
that the lover is me.
it's as if i am naked
laying flattened
in my ash puddle
of day old mentality

the lost always run

i blink
until my eyes stay open

i blink
until i can't hear

i blink
and all of sudden i'm running

i blink
and all of a sudden i'm gone

i blink onto a lingering tear
who held to my lashes for years

i blink twelve times
before i even notice

my eyes were squished close
this entire life

i blink
and i see the first house i ran to

i blink
and i see the ninth

in three years i packed and unpacked

only to realize its not where i am
but who

eagerly exposed

he's the type of person
i could write a book for
that would seem cruel to a virgin
it would be like a sixty year old macallan
in the eyes of a previous alcoholic.
it would make your teeth rot
and cause an inelegant tingle.
he's the character
who's been in the back of my head
for three years without knowing it.
before i knew him
it was already written.
he drinks his coffee black
and his whiskey on the rocks.
he lets me sleep on his chest
and we go for breakfast in the mornings.
but really i don't believe in lovers
it seems there is always a motive.
he's the type of person
who numbs the babbling poet
allowing the woman to get a word in.
what meanings are in the touch
of a man dreamt about
the type of man that can
make your clit gasp
from a gentle touch on the back
a sensation that lingers for weeks.
what kind of man would entice
a lustful gamble
for the type of woman
to bruise her spine
to the thought of him.
each touch is a scandal
weakening stubborn love

end of the storm

thunder calls
for the sun's daily conclusion
roaring
when light hits the ocean's face.
briefly consuming the day
bolts drew through somber clouds
waves close their eyes
on the salt of their tears.
indulge in the ache
of emptying filth.
pruned fingers are doomed
in the puzzle of no pieces
or constant rotation
of when they fit into place.
the suns youthful wisdom
will always dance in us,
the ocean's grace will wait.
thunder tried to call her home
he began to weep
raining a flood for a baptism
he refused to immerse in.
the sun said "let tears loose
into the end of earth
until light swings back again."
or your heart will wilt
and your days will rush.
we're doomed
in the puzzle of no pieces
don't be fooled
by the shadow of the day.
the sun will rise again
and again it will be us

baptized in the gap

i am washed
in the dirt
left purple.
right section
wrong direction
shuffling around
for the right delay of morals.
i've seen it once before
laid flat on the floor
asking god where god is
then put the response
next to my day old dinner
and a bottle of daily sacrifice;
sipping until
theres a jazzy old tune
slippery
down my ringing ears.
i am washed
purified by cognac
dismantled the belief
that silence is peace.
i never was
immured to confessions
but they wrote themselves
in my eye widened sleep.
they shimmer slightly
in the reductant glow
of heaven
as the light gets closer
i know more
about animal like impulses
in my muzzled and forsaken heart.
the monarch mind
widened gaps
to solitudes gesture of dismiss.
i was blind
to the plate of snakes
feeding the hungry fool
who would always look
for her own head

first breath

i can't write.
i've felt a kiss in the morning
and his surrender in the night.
it's so simple
to word the extension
of my body into the floor
or how the trees walk with me.
it's so simple
to word how the sun melted
into dancing jarrah branches,
how my thumb changed shapes
and had a graphic heartbeat.
i can't write now that
ecstasy was given by god,
not the city dealers
who lend a capsule
during the weekly dance;
or the poker players
who micro dose lsd in tequila.
i won't write. because
i have given myself to someone.
we exchanged our better halves
and our flaws left the ground
i wonder where they went
how long will they travel
when they're back
will they have grown up
will the ego lose its face
will i answer to my name?
i won't write
now that i recognize
the butterfly in me.
who evolved
from a stranger
in a dismay swaddle.
the stories were all wrong
butterflies don't sink in the stomach
they're in the neck
they slowly sneak up
they warm the shoulders

before falling below the waist.
heartbeat's shared
with the entire body
as if a kiss, has merged
his nerves with mine
and i can feel
how god would taste

in the house of the poet

beyond the door
words are disembodied
on the welcome mat
there's a couch on the ceiling
and cookies in the oven
resembling the smell
of fermented chilies
dipped in brown sugar.
poets poke through windows
to see the other side
when it breaks
they sweat or shiver
prior, only warmth
was served for dinner.
senses rearrange
into flecks of speech
plunge into roots of ambition.
submission
to the kettles scream
the showers delicate song
and the enemies pointed tongue.
permission
for late nights to stare
at you, from taxis ceilings
to offer you stories
offer you chances;
to entice the novice
seeking an elegant thrill.
allow them to leach
off your tingling guts.
in a wicked game made by the one
who felt too strongly
for language.
so they gathered pieces
pieces
and pieces
and pieces
just to come up with a riddle
to tamper with the criminals faith.
it's as if we all stand stiff

in the middle of a debunk.
the mirror disguised as glass
the poet knows better
than to digest
the impatient word

fragments

i remember sitting during worship on sundays
i remember praying to find my stuffed animal
i remember my first kiss while skipping class
i remember writing love poems when i was fourteen
i remember experiencing real love at twenty one
i remember the first time i did molly
i've still never smiled that much
i remember dancing in dark rooms, during sunrise
i remember little bits but really i don't remember much
i remember my long white dress bought by coke dealers
i remember begging god to start my car battery
nearly every morning, and it worked
i remember saying i'd never forget and then i did
i remember seeing my father unconscious
i remember having withdrawals in the hospital with him
i remember endless taxi rides during sunrise
i remember asking the driver if i could play afrobeat
i remember sleeping in a bed with men i couldn't look at
i remember fresh coffee and rolling a joint each morning
i remember diluted lsd in tequila
on the poker boys yacht in the summer
i remember being an hour late to work that night
and eating a burger out of my locker
i remember lusting over my manager every single shift
i remember moving in with dealers into the rich suburbs
i remember prayer flags and bamboo walls
displayed on the balcony, for moms to see
i remember riding a moped into a brick wall in bali
i remember our driver tried to drink like us
and spent the night on our back patio
i remember little bits but really i don't remember much
i remember being given a convertible beemer
i remember putting ecstasy in tea on tuesday nights
i remember taking a bath and trying to swim
i remember the layout of nine homes and three venues
i remember a few men, but none of their tastes
i remember little bits but really i don't remember much

past life

that life is now in two suitcases
a backpack and busted lip
then where am i
if i don't keep picking at it.

the past reconciles
before i got the chance
to ask why i was forgiven.
even if i glance at the battle
stability loses
and the poet revokes the pour.

oh where would i be, if i knew
where to store anarchy's devotions.
instead i pray for my lungs
that hold in distorted notions

do we ever really know
all that rots.
do we feel it turn to soil?

i wonder if we'll remember
the life outside
of what we're able to take

i partook in the devils loving
became a two headed snake
one looks backwards
and the other tries to wake.

there's memories
in every song i've ever heard

in every article of clothing
silk fabrics that don't fold well
still have fingerprints
undoing the front bow

chunky leather heels still smell like vodka
and the front door of hotel rooms.

now i am here
with rolled tobacco and bud.
undressed in silence.

eyes fixated on two suitcases
a backpack and the inability
to pull on a zipper. so i sit here
naked and cold

death in life

before i blinked,
my skin had shed

i, curled on the ground
looking at my own head

just the skull and horns
and a gentle smile

her time is done
and i am here

looking back on
what starts to clear

i'm raw to the bone
my wings have been born

the days have passed me
my youth has been worn

i embodied the devil's lover
she had too many eyes

i embodied the devil's rival
and got too close to heaven

in the shell, of a hurting woman
with too much time to sell

but here i am.
after all the writing

here i am, prepared
to start again

x

www.ingramcontent.com/pod-product-compliance
Lightning Source LLC
Chambersburg PA
CBHW022041160426
43209CB00002B/26